BREAKING THE MOLD

Why Waste Talent?

*Make a Difference and Prove It Can Be Done by
Your Decisions, Dedication & Determination*

WILLIAM E. LEE JR.

Copyright © 2013 by William E. Lee Jr.

Published by Lee's Press and Publishing Co, LLC
www.LeesPress.net

All rights reserved, including the right to reproduce this book or portion thereof in any form whatsoever.

This document is published by Lee's Press located in the United States of America. It is protected by the United States Copyright Act, all applicable state laws, and international copyright laws. The information in this document is accurate to the best of the ability of the author at the time of writing. The content of this document is subject to change without notice.

ISBN-13: 978-1-7329441-0-7
Paperback

Library of Congress Cataloging-in-Publication Data
2013906302

TABLE OF CONTENTS

Dedication 1
Acknowledgements 2
Introduction 4
Ch One: Sharing My Message: The Unbelievable Journey.
.... 6
Ch Two: The Crash.. 14
Ch Three: The Entrepreneurial Turnaround 18
Ch Four: Get Your Dream Back 24
Ch Five: Ideas Need Leaders... 31
Ch Six: The Danger of Giving Up Too Soon 40
Ch Seven: Execution is an Art 47
Ch Eight: Unlock Your Potential 59
Ch Nine: Breaking the Curse... 63
Ch Ten: Why Waste Talent.. 66
Ch Eleven: Mental Success Strategies 70
Ch Twelve: Daily Affirmations.. 72
About the Author 75

DEDICATION

First and foremost, I would like to give honor to God for all He has done for me, allowing me to stay on this earth and continuing to make a difference.

My mother, Donna Keesee, for bringing me into this world and molding me into the person I am today, by strictly raising me the right way.

My father, William E. Lee Sr, thank you for giving me wisdom and insight about life and how to walk and talk like a man.

My loving sister, Kiana Keesee (Rest in Peace) I LOVE YOU!

My grandmothers Ruby Reynolds and Marie Lee, and grandfathers Spencer Keesee, James Lee, and Rev. John Reynolds; thank you for being such inspiration and making sure I become all I can be.

Godmothers, Barbara Jean Hooper and Lutrellia McAllister; I love you for being wonderful Godmothers.

One of the best friends a man could ever have, Alfred Wooten and Wesley Poindexter.

Thanks for being great business mentor and friend, Juan Langford.

ACKNOWLEDGMENTS

To my heavenly Father who has made this book possible, I give Him all the glory. I'm certainly grateful that I'm not who I used to be, and I can't thank Him enough for giving me a good family as well as supportive mentors. They all want to see me do great things and live a life of value. He made that possible.

To my mother, thank you for raising me to be the man that I am today. You brought me up as a single mother, and I want to bless you with everything your heart desires. I'm striving to see you happier and enjoying the good life without having to struggle. You've been the best mom and I love you for that.

My grandmother Ruby Reynolds, I remember spending enjoyable nights at your house as a child. You helped raise your grandchildren in a way that was righteous and provided for our every need. You fed us not only good table food, but good food for thought. Thank you for being a wonderful grandmother.

My grandmother Marie Lee, I love you for always allowing me to be myself. Thank you for your ongoing support and being there when I needed someone to talk to about life. You always made me laugh with your funny jokes. I love you for that!

My father, I became an artist just by watching you as a child. Now, I am applying the knowledge I learned. I appreciate you for encouraging me to pursue my dreams.

My sister Kiana, I love you and will always miss you. I will always be your big brother and I'll make sure mom is taken well cared for.

I would like to thank my church family and for always being supportive in my life, and just for being great people.

Finally, to anyone else whose name I neglected to mention, thank you for everything and let's break the mold together.

INTRODUCTION

This book builds upon several life components:

- Overcoming adversity by leveraging your gifts and talents, knowledge, sharing wisdom and learning from your mistakes in life to help increase the quality of someone else's life.

- Realizing that most things happen because of the poor choices we make. You are on this earth to make a difference. The only way to make a difference is with your decisions, dedication, and determination.

- Discovering and understanding your gift to the world, *"Why Waste Talent?"* Your message, gifts and talents can open doors that will sow into your life what you reap. You can break the mold by doing things differently, destroying generational curses and embracing your uniqueness by completing tasks in such a way that others may not.

There will be times when you must put your blood, sweat and tears into what you believe in. Times you will go through trial and error and even times when you will feel like giving up. But when you finally discover your purpose, it is a life-changing event. Realize that giving up would be a selfish act and is not an option; you were created to make a difference or, *"Break the Mold"* for the sake of your legacy. Every person on this earth is distinctively different and created with a God-given talent or gift. We all possess the ability to create our own destiny, utilizing our respective strengths and weaknesses as well as unique traits and characteristics.

God plants invisible seeds in all of us; these seeds are called dreams. With the faith of a mustard seed, these dreams will flourish and manifest themselves into the physical realm. Aspirations and ambitions are placed on our hearts so that we will strive for the things we want to have, do, and become in our lifetime. You will be able to help your loved ones and others if you have passion, the will to give your all, good intentions, and consistency. When you possess all of these, the dreams that are patiently awaiting your arrival will be brought to fruition.

Have you ever had someone try to mold you into something they wanted you to be? There comes a point in your life when you have to find the fit that is right for you. Doing this starts with being yourself, not trying to be anyone else. Follow your dreams and listen to the inner voice that says you can do it and align your thoughts with your gifts and talents. You will then be in direct position to excel in business while staying true to yourself and your dreams.

As an entrepreneur, there are many things we want to accomplish at the same time. However, that is a surefire way for an entrepreneur to fail. You must stay focused on what you want to become successful in before taking on any new projects. Write down what you want to do, write the steps to achieve those goals and then act. Success in business requires a well-thought-out plan that is written clearly, one that can be strategically followed through on.

Chapter 1
SHARING MY MESSAGE: THE UNBELIEVABLE JOURNEY

The journey of a thousand miles begins with one step.

– Lao Tzu

Have you ever felt so passionate about something or someone that the situation or that person stayed on your mind constantly? The saying goes, "Never give up on something you can't go a day without thinking about." If you stay focused on taking the steps needed to achieve the goals you are passionate about, things will begin to manifest. The reason this happens is because all your positive energy is pouring into that thought. I always knew there was something inside of me that would focus on creating paths and leading others to their God-given purpose. I just did not always know how that would come to be.

I knew the source of my talents. I also knew that I have always possessed a leadership mindset. However, I was not always sure how to develop my gifts. Developing your natural gifts and talents comes from the desire to do what you love to do and would do for free; the key is to find a way to help others with your gifts and to capitalize on it. Great leaders today are using their same passion with new desires and transforming them into profitable businesses. Many of these leaders started out by working somewhere for free but in the process, they learned a skill and eventually earned a name for themselves.

After gaining a clientele, or after consistently handling business transactions, surely these leaders developed a written plan and ran full speed ahead with their vision. If you must work for someone, do so only to learn something more to become better--then work for yourself. Once you get a taste of entrepreneurship, you may never want to quit. In the entrepreneurial world, quitting should never be an option anyway. We will make mistakes; however, we must learn from our mistakes and never make the same mistake twice.

As a child, I remember the first time I saw my father drawing. I wanted to know how to draw pictures just like him. I started drawing consistently and I loved it. I was very passionate about it. One day while I was sitting at my grandmother's kitchen table drawing a sailboat in a sea, my mother came out of the back room to see what I was doing. She already knew I was artistic, but it wasn't until that moment that she realized how passionate and dedicated I was. Seeing I had potential and could maximize my talents, she said, "I need to put you in an art class." Soon after that interaction, I started my first day of class with other artists.

I fell in love with that class instantly. I cannot even explain to you how much I thoroughly enjoyed it. As time went on, I met other artists who were also very passionate about art and good at what they did. I remember meeting my art teacher for the first time and building a strong rapport with her. She was kind, generous and the coolest person you could ever meet. It felt great to be in such a welcoming, talented, and creative atmosphere with other like-minded artists.

My first piece of art was a masterpiece painting of another sailboat in the ocean. At the time, I thought it didn't have any meaning. Now I realize it may have been my vision of easy access to an abundance of joy, immunity from poverty and a sign that I was embarking on a spiritual journey. My family was very proud of me and supportive of my passion. When I expressed that I needed a nice frame to display my painting, a relative offered to buy me one. I will never forget that kind gesture. It was a bit shocking to me, and it showed me how much my relative saw the value in my work.

After being in class for a few more months, I created more pieces and framed them. But I started to think about how I could capitalize on my drawings and paintings--I came up blank. The interest I once had for drawing and painting suddenly disappeared. I decided to tell my mother I no longer wanted to pursue that in which she had already invested so much into for my future. She was disappointed, but she supported my decision.

Years later, I dreamed about being an architect, picturing myself as the owner of a company with many employees. I quickly dismissed that dream since I knew it would take quite a few years of school to make it a reality. I had an epiphany. *"I can be a graphic designer, use my creative talent and capitalize on it,"* I thought to myself. I started observing a graphic designer daily. I saw how he mastered the art for his clients, and I picked up on his skills. Once I learned how to use the tools correctly, I was again ready to focus on something that I was passionate about. I wasn't going into it because someone else wanted it for me; I was going into it because I wanted it for myself.

Here I was, a twenty-one-year-old man, pursuing his passion for art forms, while some older, more experienced individuals were still trying to find their passion. It helps to get under the wing of someone who is already where you want to be. This person must also be willing and available to mentor you on success and how to overcome obstacles you may encounter. Surround yourself with people who are not driven to impress others, but rather driven to leave a legacy for future generations. Being passionate and staying focused is highly important.

Passion comes from the heart; focus comes from avoiding distractions that may cause you to veer from the path that can take you where you want to go. To do this, you must have a reason why you want to make a difference. A reason that is so powerful, it permeates your entire mission. I look back at my past. I went from a high-school dropout to a college student, without first earning a high-school diploma. We cannot accuse anyone of the mistakes we make. We can only learn from them and make corrections.

Because of my mistakes in high school, I eventually dropped out. My mother told me that if I did not get my act together, my friends would go off to college and leave me behind. Her words became my reality. Death and life are in the power of the tongue and those who love it will eat its fruit **Proverbs 18:21**. Dropping out of school made me feel like a loser, and I was determined not to fail at anything else.

My mother spoke with my football coach and inquired

about my progress in school. The news he gave her caused her to burst into tears. That moment was the game changer for me. Immediately, I wanted to make a difference. I didn't want to see my mother cry about things that I was doing wrong. I would rather see her cry tears of joy about things that I was doing right. After a grueling process, I did earn my diploma, but not before taking college courses.

We often struggle. But it is not about how many times you struggle. It's about how many times you get back up with an abundance of unbelievable passion and focus. It was around this time when I began to realize that I was obligated to my family to be successful and break the mold. I had to change who I was associated with and what I was doing so that I would be more apt to put things in perspective

– *"You will become the equivalent of the five people you spend time with the most."*

"Never Allow Your History to Dictate Your Destiny."

Visualize where you want to be. It can be traveling the world, having a great impact on the lives of others, having money left in the bank after all debts are paid, retiring your parents, or earning multiple streams of income. Whatever your vision is, pave your way toward the manifestation of it. As the only entrepreneur in my family, I had to think outside the box. There were times when I even kicked that box to the side.

Just because I made a few mistakes in the past did not

mean my future was any less bright. Much too often, people tend to let what happened in their past keep them from overcoming and accomplishing their dreams. Always remember, our eyes are placed in front of us because it's more important to look ahead than to look back. Have you ever met someone that could explain how they wanted their future to look, and it motivated them to act? You can do the same thing. You will never know what is waiting ahead of you until you take action to get it.

"If you don't start today, you won't finish tomorrow."

Now that you know that your future is awaiting your arrival, give yourself the green light. GO! Do something different and stop worrying about where you come from. Look at what's sitting at the top level, waiting for you to reach for it. It seems that most successful people have had the toughest past you could ever imagine. But adversity didn't cause them to dim their light of perseverance and veer them off their course of action.

What are you willing to give up today that will make a meaningful change for you tomorrow? Here are a few ways to become the change you need in your life:

Look fear in the face: In business, fear does not exist. It's just an emotional response from a bad experience. Before you get past fear, you must first look it in the face and acknowledge it. I remember as a child going to bed at night with the lights on because I feared something would grab me. I knew eventually that I had to face that fear, or it would stay with me as I grew older. Today, I have no problem with sleeping in the dark. This same approach to fear applies in life or business. Go that extra mile, face your fears, and be determined that fear is not going to delay your progress.

Motivate yourself with fear: Ren Carlton said it best, "Fear is a very expensive trait to have. It's a dangerous emotion to deal with and you have to put it aside. If you don't, it will kill you. Inactivity is the worst thing you can do in the business world. You must be out there mixing it up." If you want to be the leader of a team, whether it's a business team or a sports team, you must surround yourself with those who have a reputation for using a positive mind structure. Ask questions. Tell them what your fears are. Get advice on how they overcame their obstacles. From that point on, you will be held accountable for letting go of your fears that have held you back.

Be coachable and teachable: Here is a great nugget from Vincent K. Harris: "A good friend loves you the way you are, a great mentor loves you too much to leave you the way you are." Do you see the difference? Mentors have been where you are and have faced the fear you are currently facing. Let them give you all the wisdom and insight you need so that you can apply their teachings to your everyday life or business.

I've learned these principles along the way while conducting business with people from different walks of life. When I made the decision to turn my life around, many people laughed at me and thought I was trying to be better than them. Well, that wasn't the case. I wasn't trying to be better than anyone else, but myself. My mind had outgrown my hometown, and I needed to get out and allow things to stretch in my life. I wanted to have more and do more for myself, my family, and my loved ones.

There are two things that drive people: desire and fear. I had to figure out which one was driving me the most. To be honest, it felt as though both were equally driving me at the same time. We all experience some type of fear. Fear to move into and beyond what we are called to do and the desire to become what we are destined to become. I had a desire to become a great person and to do great things. It was in my heart to reach that mark in my life. I just can't leave this earth and not make a difference. When it's my time to go, I want to say, "Father, I used everything you gave me." If you really want to achieve something great in life, push past the obstacles and tell your spirit that your family deserves better.

Chapter 2
THE CRASH

"Empty your mind; be formless, shapeless - like water. Now you put water into a cup, it becomes the cup, you put water into a bottle, it becomes the bottle, you put it in a teapot, and it becomes the teapot. Now water can flow, or it can crash. Be water, my friend."

– *Bruce Lee*

Living with my mother and not having the finances to have the freedom that I desired was challenging, to say the least. I slept on a fold-up bed that was too small. I kept my clothes in trash bags and my mind battled between where I was and where I wanted to be. I needed to get my mind off my current situation. I decided to take mom's car, without her permission, to visit a beautiful girl in a city close by. It was a rainy and dreary day, but my spirits were lifted at the thought of seeing her. I dressed with excitement and took the car keys from the kitchen counter. My visit with her proved to be a great deterrent for the moment. Driving back from seeing her, I took the Burlington exit, driving fast, yet squinting to see through the fog. There was a hit and run on the freeway. My heart pounded and I was afraid. In a hurry to return the car, I hit someone else on the intersecting ramp. The impact was shocking. But it was also a wake-up call.

I had to do the inevitable and call my mother to give her the news that her car was a now a wreck. She was more relieved that I was unharmed than she was disappointed that her car was totaled. If anything would have happened to me, she would have lost her mind. I realized that I was on this earth for a specific purpose. Though I made mistakes, I always learned from them so that I may use those experiences to help others.

This chapter outlines:

- Overcoming obstacles in life
- Helping others prevent crashes in their life
- Being determined to reach and surpass your potential

Everyone experiences a head-on collision at some point in their life, whether it is recklessness, familial disagreements or simply not having a father figure. But everyone has someone somewhere who will love them enough to keep them from crashing and burning. We have a choice to either help people clean their slate and get past the mental and emotional barriers that are holding them back or sit back and watch them waste their lives away by never leaving a legacy. How can you help someone if you haven't been through any major crashes in your life?

What do you need to do to leave a mark on the earth? The only person you are destined to *become* is the person you decide to *be*. Live in such a way that your character will precede you before you even open your mouth to speak. If life has taught you a lesson, it is now your obligation to teach that lesson to others.

In the car on my way home, I thought about the pain and hurt that I caused my mother. I felt worthless. I felt like it was a never-ending story that played repeatedly in my life.

As I was looking outside the window of the car, I couldn't see myself doing anything else but finding a solution to my problem. How could I avoid another crash? I wasn't concerned with just a car crash, but a crash that could potentially hurt others. I was determined not to be a statistic, not to let my life go to waste and not to be known as just "another one of those guys."

How will you use a crash and turn it into a positive message? A message that will help better someone else who may be going through a lot in their life? What are some things you can do to make an impact on a person's life? Do you simply hope to make a difference, or do you have a vision to be the change you want to see? There's a difference between hope and vision.

Hope is when a person has talent but doesn't apply themselves. Vision is when a person takes action because they catch a glimpse of their future. When you see someone that has talent, push them to fulfill their dreams and goals. Everyone has a dream, but is the person in the right environment and around the right type of people to bring it to fruition?

When you find something, you want to do, go do it!

Break the mold!

When you're steadily blessed with success, stay humble throughout the entire process.

Break the mold!

Your passion will take you places. Walk into what you are called to do.

Break the mold!

You have what it takes to overcome the crashes in your life.

Break the mold!

If you're tired of starting over, stop giving up.

Break the mold!

You have every right to dream big. Remove those who try to blind your vision.

Break the mold!

Never let someone distract you from achieving your goals.

Break the mold!

Everyone is not going to like you. But if you're doing the right thing, you have nothing to worry about. Remember that they didn't like Jesus either!

Chapter 3
THE ENTREPRENEURIAL TURNAROUND

"We are shifting from a managerial society to an entrepreneurial society."

– John Naisbitt

Now that you have a glimpse of my past and how I overcame certain obstacles, I will share with you how I made the shift toward change.

The purpose of this chapter is:

- To help you understand that the words you speak manifest into existence
- To show you how to tap into what is right for you
- How to make a 360° evaluation of your life and a 180° turnaround

I am passionate about empowering others with my story, letting them know that it wasn't easy to break through the most difficult times in my life. But I made a decision to change. I was inspired by this very thought, *"I will never know whose life I can change until I first change my own."* The thought of making a difference in the lives of others pushed me into action. Sometimes, that's all it takes to create change. Many people do not think before taking action. But it's how well you *think* that determines your *lifestyle*.

Has something ever bothered you to the point that you wanted to do something about it? It could be helping someone that you care about move out of a bad neighborhood. It could be a stranger on the street, freezing with no home, asking for change so he can get a meal. If it bothers you, chances are it is your purpose to extend yourself for the sake of others and end the crash in their lives. By being a servant to others, you may help steer someone in the right direction that you didn't even know was hurting.

It's never too late to make a significant turnaround. But before your life spirals too far out of control, you must be willing to remove yourself out of the equation and take the task of "breaking the mold" more seriously. The best way to accept change is to let it *grow* on you. For months while I was in school, I hung out with friends – being unproductive and wasting my time and talent. It finally dawned on me. I needed to take the time required to develop a skill I was already good at and extremely passionate about. I needed to grow into my change.

I received a letter that tuition had gone up tremendously at the university that I was attending. My mom and I couldn't afford to pay any additional expenses, so I went back home. I learned from one of my mentors that, "Every problem has a solution." I was determined not to give up. I went home disappointed because I was right back at my starting point. I knew I had to get a job and help out around the house. I began working in manufacturing companies, operating machinery, but was unfulfilled. After working those types of jobs for a few years, I realized that my talent was being wasted.

> *"Whatever lives in your mouth,*
> *lives in your future."*

While I've learned a lot in life, I realize that knowledge is only the beginning. I must also apply the knowledge. When I'm around certain people, I ask myself why they complain so much and speak negatively all the time. As I grew and my mindset began to change, I promised myself that I would speak positive words and speak wisely. I apply that knowledge daily. The words we speak are very powerful. They either create life or death. Just as you plant a seed in the ground to grow, as long as it has water, it grows--that's life. But if you stop watering the flowers, eventually they begin to wither--that's death.

It gets difficult when feelings get in the way and your mouth wants to speak what your heart feels. But with a tough mind and applied wisdom, we can avoid those negative thoughts and keep pressing. I hung around my mentors often to make sure that I learned what I knew I needed to know. Mentors are people who see your potential and guide on how to reach your goals. If you have a successful mentor and they sincerely believe in you, there's something about you that they like.

Most of them will not waste their time on someone without any potential; they will just keep leading in the process. However, everything happens in due season just as the bible states in Galatians 6:9: *"Let us not become weary in doing good, for at the proper time you will reap a harvest if you do not give up."* If you do not have a mentor who will invest time with you, it is your responsibility to strengthen your potential and seek out one. Once you have one, you do not need to like everything about them, but be grateful for them and respect them as a businessperson. I've worked many jobs in my past that I did not like, but I was grateful to have one because it allowed me to pay bills, have money in the bank, and invest in my future.

Other people may complain and speak negatively about their job that they asked for, signed the application for, and interviewed for. They may not realize they are speaking things into their life, and it causes them to become even more frustrated. I remained mentally focused by not complaining, learning from others, making sure I got the job done, and doing what I needed to do. That's how you overcome. I knew deep down in my heart that I would reap a harvest and get promoted to that next season in my life. Our brain operates off the words we speak and the images we hold in our minds. Therefore, when you can speak what you see mentally, eventually you'll see what you spoke.

If the people in your inner circle are not speaking powerful words into your life and you're not seeing significant change, then it's time to find a new circle of people. In the beginning of my growing stages, I realized what we think about manifests into our lives. It can either be beneficial to our purpose or it can become another piece of baggage that holds you back from grasping what you really want out of life. Throughout the years, I have followed the teachings of many leaders who have power and influence, such as Dr. Myles Munroe, Bishop T.D. Jakes, John C. Maxwell, Dr. Stephen R. Covey, Anthony "Tony" Robbins, and many more. The things they speak about continue to inspire me to become a better person, using everything I have in me so that I don't waste talent.

"Live with enthusiasm. Whatever you do, give it your best."

I have stated this phrase many times during conversations. Entrepreneurs thrive on having a lifelong vision and aspire to create the future not only for themselves, but for the world. The other discussion comes after they ask, "How can you possibly be the best in the *world*?" Giving your best means staying in your lane and striving to be the best in all that you do. Why would a person want to live a mediocre life and not walk in the purpose they were created to fulfill? "Knowledge is power, and enthusiasm pulls the switch" made all the sense in the world when Steve Droke stated this.

Since leaving my job, a job that wasn't for me, I immediately turned on the switch and made a significant change. It was time to get things done, have fun, gain more clients, attract more like-minded individuals, and attain better communication skills. It takes a lot of energy to be enthusiastic. If you're having trouble maintaining your drive, it might be because you need to make a change and create your own turnaround.

"Chase your dreams. Don't stay stuck in your comfort zone."

There are three types of people, and I run across them every day. There are those people who follow their dreams, those who do nothing and those who chase their dreams at full speed on a much higher level. I remember riding in the car with one of my mentors one day. We were conversing and I asked him what inspired him to go after his dreams. He said one of his mentors told him, "Don't wait until you get in your 30's and 40's and realize that you haven't accomplished anything and you're still broke." That inspired me to start chasing my dreams at full speed.

Have you ever really analyzed how you spend most of your time? When we stretch our minds to new dimensions and expand our territories, we often realize we can do more. Don't get so caught up in your comfort zone that you forget about what really matters. It's time to hit that switch and make a complete turn. Become the entrepreneur you really want to be. When life gets tough, get tougher and turn your story around. What's great about this is that you don't need to fit into the three different types of people--you can think outside the box.

Millions of people have all the potential in the world to make a complete turnaround in their lives and to help improve the lives of others. Everyone has the chance to be a person who strives for growth and self-discovery. Never stay inside a predetermined box. Make opportunities for yourself. Seek what really matters to you. Help others find their dreams and make them a reality. Jim Rohn made one of the best statements of all time when he stated, "You will have anything you WANT in life if you will help other people get what they WANT."

Chapter 4
GET YOUR DREAM BACK

"Go confidently in the direction of your dreams. Live the life you have imagined."

– Henry David Thoreau

If you have lost sight of your goals, you will have to get back into position so that you can be ahead of your game. If you can't find time to make it work, this chapter is for you.

What you will learn:

- Understanding your purpose and staying consistent in it
- Taking control of your day and blocking negative thoughts
- How to put your business first while impacting others

As an entrepreneur, there will come a point where you will feel like no one supports your vision or believes in you. Although you may have what it takes to be successful, the skills and correct mindset, there may be times when you feel incomplete. There will be times you will feel you are missing a piece that is needed to complete your puzzle. That missing piece may be your father, brother, sister, mother, mentor or perhaps a good friend. Some of those people you may have to leave behind at the start of your journey. But you can always reach out to them later.

The people who support you will be there with you every step of the way. But those who are negative and only around for what they can gain from you will only be around for a moment. To avoid being sucked into negativity, you must have unshakable focus, undeniable passion, and great mental toughness. The good thing about this is that you don't have to have everything in place at once. Pinpoint what's right for you and make an educated decision based on how you see your life unfolding. That dream is inside you. All you need to do is get your dream back and push through.

One of the reasons we experience adversity is so we may become wiser than we were before. Here are a few dynamic quotes that will give you the push you need.

"Remind yourself daily that you have what it takes."

Once start believing in yourself, the universe will get out of your way. If you are the only entrepreneur in your family or circle of friends, wouldn't you want to break the mold and show them it can be done? Break the cycle and be the one who makes a difference. It takes a person of great determination and a million-dollar mindset to take massive action. To get back the dream that seems lost, it is imperative to make a habit of reminding yourself of what's important to you. These are the things we tend to lack because of the dark clouds in our minds.

Listed here are a few reminders to help you on this journey:

You are human: This is possibly the biggest reminder of them all. You will become your own worst enemy if there's no structure in place for your life. You must have written goals and a structure to accomplish your dreams. There will be bumps along the way, and you will stumble. You may not like where this road will take you at times. But be grateful that you're not where you used to be and understand that you're still an imperfect human being.

You are in control of your own destiny: You can't completely predict which turns life will take. However, you can control the choices you make. Your choices will determine how you live your life.

You have to find a hiding place away from the world: Sometimes, you need to go into your hiding place, away from the rest of the world. This allows you to regain focus on your dreams. Cluttered minds cannot function well. But if you're still, your mind conjures up and brings your dreams to fruition.

Never, ever, ever, give up: When you're close to what you're about to achieve, don't give up; go further. Keep going until you reach your mark and check off that goal.

> *"Your reason why should be so powerful; it changes you from who you used to be."*

What do you think you were put on this earth to do? Whose life do you want to change for the better? What is your legacy? Once we identify our purpose in life, we can then lead ourselves to our true destiny. One of my mentors once told me, "Your destiny is attached to someone else's." In other words, during the journey to your destiny, you must help someone else get to their own destiny. You must have at least one strong reason why you want to make a difference, and it should be able to spark determination in you every time you think of it. Keep this in mind and it will inspire you to lay out your game plan and take action toward accomplishing your goals.

My reason *why* is my family and the legacy I will leave to future generations, including the children I have yet to be blessed with and their children. Although I went to college without a high school diploma, the dean emphasized that I must have my diploma before the semester ended in order to continue college. Well, I made the decision to move forward. With my dedication and determination, I earned my diploma and walked across the stage with a proud look on my face. My family was proud of me as well. The look on their faces seeing me walk across that stage was priceless. It was like an inauguration of greater things to come, the first step to breaking many molds.

"On the road to success, you will make many mistakes."

The most common mistake people make is making the same mistake multiple times. The definition of insanity is doing the same thing over and over again and expecting different results. We should be able to learn from our mistakes, gain wisdom from them, and not allow ourselves to make the same mistakes repeatedly. Even leaders make mistakes, but a great leader learns from each one. The same thing applies to certain people in your life who may have wronged you. Get past the things you perceive they have done to you. Stop trying to get revenge and start working on what you're passionate about.

Do you pay attention to how you spend your time? Since getting my dream back, I learned how to manage my time much more wisely and stay focused. It is a huge disservice to you if you are scattered between ideas and putting your energy into all of them at once. You won't get anywhere fast doing that. Getting what's rightfully yours requires logical thinking, good timing, and unwavering focus. If you find yourself thinking heavily about vacations, watching television, being on social media just to socialize every hour on the hour, your business plan, and family issues, how can you stay focused, dedicated, and determined to make your dream a reality?

Some people pray before getting up, while some just get up and get their day started. I'm not perfect, so there were many days where I forgot to pray. But most of the time, I pray before getting my day started. Your purpose is who you are, not what you do. What you do could be your talents, but who you are is what's in your heart and what you desire. No one can take away what you have been called to do but *you*. Knowing what you are called to do and being consistent in bringing it to fruition is important. Eventually, you will see results.

One of my mentors taught me to jot down affirmations and read them aloud while brushing my teeth. If you do this daily, you will start to see a dramatic change in your life. It has been proven that if you write down the things that you want in your life, they will have a much higher chance of materializing. You will find samples of daily affirmations in the final chapter of this book. Take control of your day by speaking into the atmosphere and attract what you desire.

This is how your brain works: you speak aloud what it is that you want. Your brain listens and immediately starts working toward making it happen for you. Whatever you focus on, you attract, and it will show up for you because you spoke it into existence. But you must be careful what you focus on. Simply saying aloud, the opposite of what you want will attract what you don't want. For example, if you want to be a millionaire, say, "I am a millionaire." Never say, "I am broke."

Doing so will attract poverty into your life. This is where you will need mental toughness. Block out what's causing you to steer in the opposite direction of where you want to be. If you follow these simple steps every day, you will experience a shift in your life. Be consistent.

Consistency to purpose requires focus. Therefore, you want to focus on your primary goals and take decisive, immediate action. Don't set goals that are too big. Instead of setting a goal to learn three new languages within a year, set a goal to immerse yourself in social settings with people who speak one language you want to learn. If you do this consistently, you will learn to speak the language naturally.

During this transformation process, become a person who is productive, but never too busy to appreciate your journey. Change the blueprint if you must. Many people try to aim for perfection when reaching toward their goals. But excellence (not perfection) is the key to getting things accomplished. Spend time with the people who are already where you want to be professionally and personally. This will create a balance in your life so that you will be able to motivate and inspire others while you inspire and motivate yourself.

Chapter 5
IDEAS NEED LEADERS

From the last chapter, were you able to see yourself so far into the future that it made you want to push and take action toward it? The idea is to separate from your past by creating a brand new you, worthy of the future you desire. Imagine how good it is going to feel when you're no longer where you used to be. You're either a leader or you are becoming a leader. Wherever you are in your journey, the ideas inside the dark room of your mind need a leader.

Most entrepreneurs who are serious about success can visualize their ideas, but some of them don't write them down. Therefore, they will sometimes lose an idea that could change their lives and the lives of others. There is power in a dedicated person who sees their vision and writes it down.

This chapter covers:

- Overcoming mental wars and challenges
- Taking full responsibility and capitalizing on your ideas
- The role of a powerful servant leader

Key Principle #1

"Our biggest battles are never physical; they're mental."

Mental motivation is something that comes from within. It separates the highly successful entrepreneur from the merely good one. It separates the person who only wishes from the person who takes action. A person without mental motivation can have all the natural talents or abilities, and yet not make it as far as someone with average abilities. Ideas and so-called leaders come a dime a dozen. What separates those who are true leaders from the rest is the ability to turn an idea into a legacy, the desire to change the lives of others, and firm belief in one's own future.

Winning in the business world is a mental process, a war even at times. One must be mentally fit when developing strategies to win the battle. History tells us that significant mental power has shaped the future of people, organizations, and even nations. Look at great leaders such as Bill Gates, Steve Jobs, Oprah Winfrey, Michael Jordan, and Martin Luther King, Jr. They stuck with an idea with purpose in mind. None of them allowed challenges or distractions to get them off track; they transformed nations and changed the world.

Key Principle #2

"S.M.A.R.T. ~ Success Means Achieving Results Together."

Have you ever taken on a task, but knew there was no way possible that you could do everything without help? John Boyd said it best, "People, Ideas, and Technology" in that order. He was simply stating that professional leadership is contingent upon the core set of ideas concerning who we are, where we are headed, and the set of values and principles that guide our journey. Collectively, this forms a leadership philosophy expressed in our choices, actions and behavior.

When making business decisions, having a team to help lead an idea will add more value. When there's a solid foundation to build on, your team will bring thoughts and ideas to the company that perhaps you may not have thought of. As a result, everyone contributes to the expansion of the company, yet has full responsibility over their own actions.

Key Principle #3

"Always do your best. What you plant now will harvest later."

Augustine "Og" Mandino was right on the money with this statement. Difficult times will come but remember that there is something waiting for you that is just for you. Go for it and remember your legacy depends on what you do today. The world operates on principles and actions. If a thought or idea is not acted on immediately, it has a greater chance of disappearing. I find it difficult to understand how some individuals have a vision for their lives yet won't move on it quickly.

What if you were the one person who thought of an idea, acted on it immediately, and it changed the history of future generations? What if acting on that idea changed your current situation, and you didn't have to work a traditional job for the rest of your life? You must take action on what you believe in, even if you fail. I learned this from Vincent K. Harris: "You can't expect to reap a harvest in something you haven't sown into."

Key Principle #4

"The mind is like a paintbrush. It can color any situation."

Your thoughts are influenced by the books you read and the people who you associate with. But you are not always influenced in a direct manner. Sometimes, people can be vicariously influenced by the teachings, actions, and/or the mistakes of others. Allow the mind to absorb experiences and use those experiences to paint the picture for your life. If you surround yourself with negativity, you will learn negative habits. Gary Coxe said, "Never allow someone to rent space in your head." Especially if they aren't influencing you to be better and do better. The mind is so powerful that if you master what you don't know, you can teach it to your team and organizations; doing this will bring about productive change. Remove the mental clutter. Disassociate yourself from people who are distracting. Discipline yourself and focus. An impaired mind cannot paint a promising future.

An impaired mind brainwashes you to believe:

- You can't accomplish anything, allowing you to believe what others think about you.
- You can't think for yourself.
- You are lacking in your goals and desires.
- You do not need to follow your daily affirmation agenda and apply it.

- You don't have to take the important steps to better your future.

Once you decide that enough is enough, it is then time to get refocused. A business is the reflection of its owner and how it is operated. Replace your impaired thinking with thoughts of success and prosperity.

Say to yourself:
- I have what it takes to be successful.
- I stay away from people who slow my process.
- I am around power people who can shorten my learning curve.
- I will have a set schedule for my future, and I am sticking to it.
- I have balance in my life.
- I am focused on personal growth for the next level in life and business.

Now take action!

Key Principle #5

"When you focus on today, you will be ready for a great tomorrow."

Although tomorrow is not here yet, when we focus on what needs to take place today, we will be better off tomorrow. Many people get anxious about tomorrow and can't prioritize what needs to be completed today. When you're disciplined and determined to do what it takes today, you will be well prepared for tomorrow. If you read Matthew 6:34, it states, *"Do not worry about tomorrow, for tomorrow will care for itself."* Some people are more prone to worry than others. But worrying is a waste of time and can be prevented.

Key Principle #6

"As we are thinking and speaking, we are creating."

If you don't understand this principle in life and business, you will continue to welcome failure by attracting into your life the things you do not want. Have you ever been in need of a job and willing to take any job? A few months later, you get a call for a position, and everything sounds okay during the interview process. However, when you start the new position, you realize it's not something you like or you're passionate about. Remember, you must be specific when you're seeking manifestation.

Many people don't take the time to be specific in what they want. They allow their emotions to drive them, and they usually end up in uncomfortable situations. Working on something you don't enjoy means you're simply wasting talent. Use wisdom. With an expanded mindset, you'll know exactly what you want. Start a business doing something that ignites your passion and drive. Confess the following:

- I want to start a business working for myself, but I need to get a job that I'm passionate about to fund my dreams.

- I have created a written plan to map out my future success and will present it to investors who are liable.
- Lord, enlarge my territory and bring the right people into my life that see my vision.
- I am winning in the race of life.
- I will prosper and become wealthy as my business takes off so that I may better help others.

Key Principle #7

"You never know whose life you will change, until you first change your own."

Change comes from within; no one can change a person but themselves. When I started hanging around different people who had the same desires and mindset that I had, my mindset started to expand. I eventually outgrew where I came from because I wanted more out of life. Ideas began to pop up in my mind, and as they were popping up, I started writing them down. So, when I started working on that idea, I could refer back to that piece of paper.

Learning was a process, and I always knew that if I focused on an amount, it would be for just that moment; however, when focusing on an idea, it was for a *lifetime*. Never become so comfortable with yourself that you forget that the ideas you have can possibly change everything else around you. But you first have to want to change yourself. How can a person change the world and never change himself? It isn't possible. Change is always a good thing; you just have to want it for yourself and everyone else as well. "You are one thought away from changing the lives of your family." This is how great leaders think in order to create generational wealth.

Key Principle #8

"Every business has the potential to become a great enterprise."

If you want to know where you'll be in five to 10 years from now, just listen to what you talk about the most. "Your tongue is a rudder." Since we are embarking on that next step, I want to clearly state that all you have to have is a dream, a strong back bone, a plan to build something great, along with dedication and determination. After studying and learning the secrets on how Oprah Winfrey, Henry Ford, Aliko Dangote, Bill Gates, John D. Rockefeller, Mark Zuckerberg, J. Paul Getty and Mark Cuban became so successful, I realized it really wasn't a "secret" at all.

In fact, most of them are school dropouts, yet billionaires. This proves that all you need is the will to make good decisions, couple with dedication and determination. I'm a fan and owner of many personal development and business books. In the book *Make Today Count*, John Maxwell highlighted, "The secret to your success is determined by your daily agenda."

Throughout our lives, we meet people who over exaggerate yesterday, overestimate tomorrow, and underestimate today. In today's world, we tend to focus on the economy too much and complain too often about yesterday. We tend to have big plans of what we will do tomorrow but the fact is, we forget about the importance of today. Whatever it is you do, don't allow your ideas to go to waste. Stand firm as a bona fide leader on what you believe in.

Chapter 6
THE DANGER OF GIVING UP TOO SOON

"When You Feel Like Giving Up, Remember Why You Held on For So Long in the First Place"

- *Unknown*

Many people give up. Others realize that if they give up on their dreams, they will never see them in their future. You have to see the big picture and move beyond what you thought you were capable of doing. That's how you grow. Always remember this philosophy: "If you don't have rain in your life, you can't *grow*." Things don't always come easy. But when you make good decisions, are dedicated to your goals, and determined to win, you won't give up easily.

As a leader, you have to take full responsibility for what you do because there are people in your circle who are counting on you and watching your every move. Stop taking the wheel all the time. Allow God to drive you through life. Free your mind from the poverty mindset and create an abundance mindset. Many people blame the recession for their financial problems, but the only recession is in your mindset. You can master anything once your mind decides to overcome.

In this chapter, I will share the things that you are still held accountable for, even if you decide to give up on your process:

- Legacy motivation

- How many lives you could possibly change?
- Changing your family's history and future generations
- Giving back
- Fulfilling God's purpose
- Leading someone else to their destiny
- Helping others avoid mistakes

Maybe some of these things are irrelevant to you. But if you are reading this book, you are a leader and you will either lead others to their success or their devastation. The choice is yours. For every check point above, you can change someone else's life and even your own in the process. Here's how:

- Inspiring your family and making a significant change to take them to new levels in life
- Changing lives and helping solve problems Making a difference in your community
- Fulfilling God's purpose
- Helping others shorten their learning curve
- Helping ensure that others don't make the same mistakes twice

Life is full of tests. The test is to see how you handle certain situations. Either they make you stronger or make you throw in the towel. The key is to figure out what's important to you and make it work. If your plan doesn't work, come up with a different strategy or seek the advice of mentors. Mentors are just like road maps; they are designed to teach and guide you through certain areas in life.

You only have three choices in life: give up, give in, or give it all you've got. It is important that you don't give up too soon.

Top 7 Reasons You Should Never Give Up

Your family and friends: Put every effort into pursuing your dreams. There's at least one person in your family who is counting on you to make a difference.

Your legacy: What is your legacy? What is something so great and important that you want to leave it to your children and their children? Dedicate time to creating your legacy; doing this is more important than giving up.

Happiness: Every time you have the urge to give up, send a positive signal to your mind telling it that it can accomplish anything. Change your thinking.

There are people worse off: Look at your life right now and look at someone else's life that has it worse than you. Right now, someone is wishing they could have what you have.

You are too close: Look at how far you've come. You have everything you need to fulfill your destiny. Stop making excuses and just make it happen.

You deserve the best: Don't settle for less. Settling is telling your spirit that you don't deserve better. When you do this, you are lowering your standards.

Talent is your gift back to God: I love this quote by Leo Buscaglia: "Your talent is God's gift to you; what you do with it is your gift back to God." I've often heard that if you don't use your gifts and talents, they will be taken away from you. Are you maximizing your gifts and talents?

It takes a mindset change to overcome giving up too soon. Nine years ago, I chose to go a different route than the crowd. I knew that if my thinking changed, my life would change. You have an obligation to fulfill your purpose because your dreams have been planted into your heart by the Creator. If you do not fulfill these dreams, a burden will settle on your heart until you complete the purpose God designed you for.

People tend to give up on their dreams, not because they don't have what it takes, but because of the people they spend time with. Put your dreams and goals back in your heart because one day, you will wake up and there won't be any more time to do the things you've always dreamed of. The key to success is persistence; the only thing that is stopping you is *yourself*.

Many have told me that some of the people in their circle or their family don't support their dreams, which causes them to get frustrated and lose sight of what they want to accomplish. I went through the same situation. My friends used to laugh and joke about what I wanted to do, but I didn't let that stop me. I rose above the ridicule and was determined to succeed because I believed in myself. That is something you have to do as well. Here's a quote I live by day to day: "Success is not an option; it's a mandatory meeting."

Imagine that you're on your job and the manager calls a mandatory meeting for all employees. You have to be there; if you miss this mandatory meeting, you could be penalized or possibly lose your job. It's the same way with success in your life and business. You have to be willing to make progress. The major factor in making progress is the *mental* side. Consider the following statement:

"I've failed a lot in my life, but the thought of giving up never existed. You have to keep your mind leveled to where it's mentally focused and away from all the distractions, mental clutter, disappointments, hurt, depression, and discouragement. Always remember, our greatest battles are not physical; they're *mental*."

The same principle is used for successful name brands. Consider how major corporations and individuals stuck with what they believed in. They built a team of already motivated individuals who believed in one vision, one brand, one company, which inspired them to go further and find every solution to any problems that surely came about. I've been guilty of giving up too soon in life. But I didn't allow my mind to be cluttered. Family, friends, things, objects, and even colleagues will discourage you from going after what you really want in life.

If you don't have something to look forward to, such as bold dreams and a big future, then your soul isn't being nourished. Les Brown stated, "You've got to be hungry." You have to take responsibility and develop a hunger for success to achieve your dreams. What do you do when you're hungry? You *eat*. It's the same way with success. If you get hungry for it, you will find a way to have it.

"It doesn't matter where you've been; it only matters where you're headed."

The key in life is to keep looking toward your future; however, if you don't take action, you will stay in the same place. Most people say, "I have a bright future," but then they sit on their butts and hardly ever apply themselves in life to become a better person. Commit yourself to lifelong learning. The greatest asset in life is the peace of mind of knowing what you have, what you want to accomplish, and having a circle of supporters who are loyal and trustworthy. If you gave up today, what would things look like for you in the future?

In today's world, people no longer value persistence, preparation, dedication, and determination. When one stumbling block comes our way, we often want to give up and quit in the process. Sometimes teenagers will quit school just eight weeks before graduation when, in all honesty, they can make it if they keep focused just a little while longer. My story was slightly different. I didn't drop out because I *wanted* to give up. Dropping out was the result of my poor choices. But because of these choices, I ended up giving up on myself too soon.

When Michael Jordan got cut from his high school basketball team, of course he was heartbroken and devastated. But after that, he was determined to create his own future. He simply went in his backyard and mastered the game of basketball. Now today, look at his brand and legacy he's leaving for his children and future generations. He went from adversity to overcoming and broke the mold. What if MJ decided to just give up and work a traditional job? This same motivation applies to you. Never give up too soon.

Chapter 7
EXECUTION IS AN ART

You can't afford to waste talent. You must learn to execute your ideas because time waits for no one. Execution can be quite difficult and draining at times, but don't take "No" for an answer. Never make excuses as to why you can't accomplish your goals. People's visions often die because of the lack of taking action, funding, and lack of business knowledge. What's holding up your execution?

Some people often find every possible way to think of why they *can't* do something instead of figuring out a solution to do it. Don't let what you *can't* do, prevent you from what you *can* do. Once you switch your thinking, everything else starts to find its way toward you. However, you *must* make the decision to execute.

If working in the corporate sector isn't for you, at least stretch your mind to having a corporate mindset. It doesn't matter if you are in the urban field, a gospel artist, or a college student. I believe entrepreneurship is about starting somewhere. It can, it does, and it should start at a young age. What we learn early stays with us for life.

Here are some mistakes young entrepreneurs tend to make:

- Acting on their emotions and not consulting with someone who's specialized in that field

- Not realizing that business is business and personal is personal
- Not having a mentor that's in the same field or realm of business
- Making money and not using portions to fund back into their projects
- Not implementing dynamic strategies and planning properly
- Wasting time and resources

Here are some steps you should execute:
- Sit down with a mentor who has the same mindset and/or has studied the industry that you're in
- Build a team or get in a quiet area to lay out a detailed game plan for your product or business
- Implement strategies as if the funds for execution are already available
- Don't let your emotions take over your passion
- Start the process

Everyone is unique in their own way. What works for others simply doesn't work for everyone else. But sometimes, we stop ourselves from achieving things because we get in our own way.

In Chapter 4, I spoke about reading affirmations daily. When I wake up, I have to give God prayer and thank Him. I've learned to never wake up without thanking God for everything He has done. I often find that reading my affirmations and speaking them into existence five times a day helps draw a passionate force. That force drives me to get things accomplished.

> ***"Anyone can steal ideas, but no one can steal execution or passion."***

Execution and passion go hand in hand. You can't have one without the other. You need to have the willpower to execute something based on a thought. You need passion to go out and make it happen. It is empowering to be able to step out of your comfort zone and do something different than from what everyone else is doing. You aren't just powerful, but you are *power* itself. You are more than capable of making things happen.

Many people aren't motivated to bring to life what they really want to do. Some who do may start off small, and others start off with the process of doing things on a larger scale because they have done their research. It's okay to be unique in your execution because the way you execute is unlike anyone else. The person who said, "Be yourself, everyone else is taken" was exactly right.

Over the years of doing business, I've learned these five critical components that every individual or company needs:

Business Plan

A well-written business plan includes a good marketing plan and knowing your target audience. The most common mistake is not doing your research. If you don't know anything about a business plan, do your research and hire someone to write the plan. "People who fail to plan, plan to fail."

Money

Your dreams don't stop just because you don't have the money. If you're working a job, make sure you put monies to the side to start your own business. Remember, your business reflects you. You usually have to be in business for two years in order to get a loan from the bank. However, do not skip step 1. You will need a business plan to get a loan for sure.

Website, Logo & Marketing Materials

You must have a brand that catches the eye of your target audience; if you don't, you lose. Marketing your business and building a brand name is not just for big companies; it starts with you as an individual. Branding your business is as important as growing your company, big or small. Repetition, consistency, and visibility are the keys to building a successful brand. Below are branding materials you will need.

Branding: A brand can be defined as, "a name, logo, slogan, and/or design scheme associated with a product or service." If you are in business today, it's imperative that you brand your business with a first-rate logo, website, business cards, letterhead, print ads, etc.

Logo: A logo should be effective, an eye opener, and able to brand you and whatever it is that you do. It affects your business just as a person is the reflection of their company. Just look at some of the big-name brands such as Verizon, Sprint, Dell, Apple, and Microsoft. They all have one thing in common: simplicity.

Website: Many people say your website is your online presence. But in many cases, it's also your online business card. Having your logo presented on every page of your website shows that your company is consistent. Have you ever seen websites that look too busy? It should look clean and professional. Once you have a clean, professional look, then it's time to promote.

Business Cards: Business cards are your tools to approach other professionals and introduce yourself. Make sure your logo is displayed properly and that your card includes your contact information and your company's address. If you work from home, never include your home address. Your first impression is your last impression.

Letterhead: Be sure to include your logo, company name and contact information in your letterhead. All of your branding should coordinate and be consistent across the board.

Strategies for Social Networks: Many people are using social networking sites to promote their business. They are FREE, so why not use them?

Most social networking sites can be used to target a specific audience. Make sure you know where your audience is located. Create strategic plans to promote yourself, a product, or service. If you look at the major people who are making money, impacting lives, inspiring individuals, and providing good content, they are building relationships. Nurturing relationships is the key to build your business and marketing your brand.

> *"There are two things that don't work well when they're closed: a parachute and a closed mind."*

Imagine getting off a plane. You're about to skydive. You are wearing a parachute and you jump off. Can you feel the intensity? Now imagine the parachute not opening. It remains closed. What are you going to do now? Picture in your mind the same thing, but this time you jump off and the parachute opens. You feel much better because you can guide safely through the air.

When you have an open mind, you can guide yourself in such a way that you attract opportunities. When your mind is closed, you prevent opportunities from coming your way. It means you're preventing yourself from achieving the most out of life. Keep your mind open to new possibilities because there's so much more that this world has to offer and it's a terrible thing to waste talent.

> *"A good attitude will open more doors than your talent will."*

The one thing I tell my mentees is that people don't buy products and services, they buy *people*. Once you understand this concept, you'll know exactly how it works. Mark Twain said it best: "People only do business with who they know, like and trust." If you're in business, it just makes sense. Believe it or not, everyone is not going to like you. Some people are not going to do business with you for multiple reasons. But you cannot dwell on them. Move on to the next person or opportunity.

Hiring someone for their services alone or buying their

products is not why people tend to do business with them. It's the fact that they know, like or trust them, which is crucial in expanding your business. Some people think they can attend events, mingle in the community, shake a few hands, pass out a business card or two, and everything flows well. In most cases, it takes a little bit more effort than that. You never know who is watching and testing you to see how well you build networks and relationships. Once people know, like and trust you, they will want to do business with you.

I was at networking event where I witnessed three gentlemen who came in from another city, two of which had no clue what networking was all about. The first gentleman approached me and introduced himself. He gave me a short speech about what he did and then proceeded to go to the next person. The second one shook my hand, handed me his promotional materials, and didn't bother to give his name. But the last one introduced himself, shook my hand, had the correct posture, and started an ordinary conversation.

Instead of giving a spiel about himself, he asked me what I do professionally. Now, that is how you build relationships. I would do business with this man because he obviously is knowledgeable about how to conduct himself professionally. Any business savvy person would not do business with the other two individuals. Their character and attitude tell a lot about how they handle business.

"Many people take advice, but only the wise will profit from it."

Have you ever received business advice at a seminar, boot camp, conference, or just out in a local public place where professionals congregate and network, such as Panera Bread or Starbucks? Did you take the advice given to you and run with it? In other words, did you make a profit off it? There's an art to taking advice. The advice you soak in could be the very next thing you use to grow your business. Find opportunities to soak in value from others. Think about how you're going to serve people with it, as well as how you can capitalize on it.

Never waste talent because it will stay with you if you use it properly, and it will line up with your purpose. Skills, talent and purpose are three different things. Let's take a look at what these three things are. Skills are learned from doing something consistently. Everyone you associate with has some type of skill. It can be writing, speaking, dribbling a ball or even being a salesperson. Many people have various skills and are known for doing all of them very well. However, everyone who has a skill may not want to use that skill to make a living because it does not align with their purpose.

When trying to find your purpose and identify your talents, consider not only what you are good at, but what you would do for free every day, all day for the rest of your life. Will it help others, and can you capitalize on it? If you can figure that out, it's your passion and your purpose. For example, a person who has a talent for speaking can offer free speaking events and pursue becoming a successful public speaker. Since they are passionate about it, it will become their business, as well as allow them to fulfill their purpose.

Taking advice and running with it takes the speaker from where he is now to where he is destined to go – speaking at large conferences, events, and seminars around the globe. It's not about the profit; it's about how he is going to impact lives and give value to others who attend these events. If you're a new entrepreneur, it would serve you well to apply the information you just learned. Not new to the business world? Pass the information along to someone who is new and aspiring to shape their future.

Starting a business can be overwhelming, frustrating, and downright tiring. But it is worth it to see your vision appear right before your eyes. Never go at it alone. Always consider logical business advice so that you may avoid mistakes others have made before you. Since I am certainly not the only businessperson with sound advice, I reached out to a few business associates in my network and asked for their advice for new entrepreneurs. These people include business experts, entrepreneurs, business owners, clients, and great speakers. Below you will see their comments!

Get to know your partners: Building relationships is the most important part of starting a business and sustaining it. Building great relationships helps take your business to another level. Successful entrepreneurs understand that getting to know people is more important than just meeting people.

Thanks to: Juan Langford, (Professional Speaker, Business Coach)

Become unemployable: If you start a process and it fails, there is no plan B. There can be a plan B within plan A. Do whatever it takes to *not* work for someone else and build a business.

Thanks to: Gary Coxe, (Entrepreneur and Public Speaker) www.GaryCoxe.com

Do it afraid: Your dream, goal, and ambition of being an entrepreneur is going to be met head on with fear. Will it work? Will you make it? What will others think? My best advice is to do it afraid. Look fear in the eye and meet it head on. You won't have all the answers at first, but you will learn. Zig Ziglar said, "You don't have to be great to get started, but you have to start to be great."

Thanks to: Tim Davis, (Business Coach and Speaker) www.TimDavisOnline.com

You are your message. Perfect it daily: When developing a business, especially as a speaker, you must work on leading yourself well before you can start and grow a business that involves leading others. Therefore, work on becoming the best you that you can be - an original - nothing less. Allow the way you live and conduct business to be the loudest message your audience will hear.

Thanks to: Lakeisha McKnight, (Award-Winning Entrepreneur and Speaker) www.lmcknight.com

Know your target market inside and out: So many entrepreneurs do a great job of identifying their area of expertise by taking the time to gain industry knowledge in the beginning stages of their business. It is a big mistake in not knowing and understanding the true needs of your target market. You can have a great product, even offer a great service. But if your product or service does not meet the needs of your specific target market, then the likelihood of success is slim to none. Take the time to know who your target market is, where they are, what they need, and how you can meet that need. An entrepreneur's focus should always be to solve their customers' problems and/or meet their needs in a way that their competitors cannot.

Thanks to: Yolanda Moore, (Two-time WNBA Champion, Author, and Speaker)

www.ymoore33.com

The power of cash flow: For many of us who start a business, our goal is to accumulate and set aside as much money as possible. This is called managing cash flow, which is the most powerful financial concept in the world. It is the amount of your cash flow, not your salary, which will determine how successful you will be in life. Cash flow is not simply your ability to make money, but also your ability to manage and multiply it. Again, the key is not how much you make, but how much of what you make is kept and not given to your creditors. At this point, you should be asking yourself, "What is cash flow and why is it so important?" Cash flow is simply your inflows (money from your business salary and assets) minus your outflows (debts, living expenses and play money). The difference in those two is what's called cash flow. It's this number, and this number alone, that will determine the quality of your life. Your decision to acquire assets is based on the cash flow you receive. Be mindful, you are not trying to purchase the most expensive asset or the property that is in the right neighborhood, but rather assets that produce cash flow. In life and in business, every single financial decision a person makes must be made considering this question: "How will this decision impact my cash flow?"

Thanks To: Vincent K. Harris, (Investor, Mentor and Entrepreneur)

www.VinceOnBusiness.com

Be yourself when applying every piece of advice that's given to you so that you may become that consummate businessman or businesswoman you've always wanted to become. The future is yours!

Chapter 8
UNLOCK YOUR POTENTIAL

Progress equals promotion. So far, I hope I have inspired you to use everything you've been given to succeed in the entrepreneurial world. You can make a difference in this world with the decisions you make, the dedication you show and the determination you have. Take this with you today as you move forward toward your destiny: "Your dreams are seeds that live inside of you; just don't let them be buried with you."

Without a doubt, always be the person you want to meet in life and in business. It's time to make a change and decide that you want to leave a Godly legacy for years to come. Your achievement begins in your mind. The NBA was in someone's mind. Apple was in Steve Jobs' mind. You have to think outside the box. Your quality of life will be more refreshing when you see the vision.

Even if it takes a while, it's better to reach your potential now before it becomes a much longer process later. Use your message to your advantage and for the advancement of others. How can a person change where they are going before they change what they are looking at? It all comes with the way you view yourself. That comes with your body language and the confidence you have.

Make up your mind that you're going to break the mold by doing things differently, unlike anyone else. Be diligent in your work and live by the attitude of "Just do it." Never give up on anything you believe in. I'm excited to know that you are willing to unlock every door in your life and utilize your potential. You need to succeed so that you will stand firm and grow your business, help someone in your family and make a huge impact on the lives of many. You have a great mindset. Just stay around other people who are dedicated to their future and who want to go far in life.

Refer this book to the people you encounter every day. Encourage others that you know need inspiration to get a copy for themselves and go after great things in life. I truly believe that it's not about creating more followers, but about creating more leaders. It took me years to finally sit down and write this book, to tell the story of how I was a high school dropout and initially got into college without a high-school diploma. What life taught me in general is that you have to lock in on your dreams. It does not matter what the naysayers think, say, or do. People will doubt your potential and only see you as the person you *used* to be.

Don't let them slow down your progress. Just keep pushing toward your ideal future and remember, "Your future is created by what you do *today*, not *tomorrow*." When you don't let the small things get to you, it simply means you're growing. Keep dreaming and moving forward. But move while you're dreaming so that you're able to unlock the potential that's on the inside of you. Surviving is not enough. You have to live your biggest dreams, make sure you don't waste talent and *break the mold.*

Unlocking Your Potential:

Be motivated: You should be the first to rise each and every day, getting up before your family and friends. Without motivation, you can't do it. Quiet the mind throughout your day. When you have a still mind, you can do anything. Here are a few motivational tips:

- Say your daily affirmations before working on your plans.
- Identify what it is you really want to accomplish. Write them down on paper and be as detailed as possible with the steps you will take to finish every goal.
- Write down who you need to help you achieve each goal and a deadline you expect to finish.
- Seize your day and keep your mind focused.

Prioritize time: Putting your priorities in line is critical. You can't regain the time you've lost from being distracted.

- Whatever you feed the most grows the most. Make sure you feed into your goals and dreams and watch how much they grow.
- Act on your potential. Money loves speed.
- Lay out your daily tasks by scheduling a certain time for each one.

Take action: Based off your list that you have prioritized, take step-by-step actions so that you will start to see results from each action point.

Unbelievable focus: Distraction and procrastination are two of the main reasons most people can't get anything done. A long time ago, I used to have trouble with focusing. But when I began to discipline myself, I started to see a lot of potential in me. There are going to be distractions everywhere (cell phones, cluttered environments, social media, TV, etc.). But to avoid lack of focus, you have to constantly tell yourself to stay on task.

Personal development: In order to become the person, you want to become, you have to change and work at being a better person. No one can change you, but *you*!

Self-image/posture: How well you present yourself tells a lot about you. Don't waste your potential by not having the correct posture. Always see yourself as a winner. See yourself as already being successful and a finisher. For if you change the way you see yourself, you'll rise to a new level. You will never rise any higher than the image you have of yourself.

Know your strengths and weaknesses: Some people do not know their strengths and weaknesses. You can find out by asking ten people who are close to you. However, I'm sure you have heard the saying, "Be careful who you share your weaknesses with. Some people can't wait for the opportunity to use them against you." You can't share all of your weaknesses with certain people. Some of them will try to use your weaknesses to stop you from growing. Be sure to work on them and adopt a different mindset toward your success.

Chapter 9
BREAKING THE CURSE

"You are the one that's going to have to break this curse," were the life-changing words little Christopher heard his aunt say to him. He didn't know what they meant at the time. But he did know it meant some kind of *change*.

One day, he and his family were sitting on the sofa in the living room. There were some familial issues being discussed and emotions were at their peak. There was a lot of confusion and Christopher could not understand just what was going on. But he wanted to know how he could help fix it. From that point on, he knew exactly what he had to do. Christopher needed to be the change his family needed. Have you ever heard of a self-fulfilling prophecy? Well, those words helped shape Christopher's future and the future of generations to come. He now understands that in order to break a cycle, you cannot accept the unfavorable as just a way of life. He also learned that complaining about and simply tolerating a situation can never change it. In essence, if you tolerate something you do not like, you are accepting it into your life. Is there a difference between tolerance and acceptance?

Until people realize that there isn't any difference between the two and raise their standards, they will continue to wallow in mediocrity. Do you know someone who has always worked hard for their loved ones, yet never really have enough to enjoy life? They pass this trait on to their offspring, and the trait is handed down to the third and fourth generations. This is a generational curse. Someone who recognizes the trend, but doesn't do anything to stop it, doesn't desire change for future generations. Christopher was determined to break his generational curse.

The Bible mentions generational curses in several places. Namely, Exodus 20:5, 34:7; Numbers 14:18; and Deuteronomy 5:9. God warns us that He is, "a jealous God, punishing the children for the sin of the fathers to the third and fourth generation of those who hate me." Do you think it sounds unfair for God to punish children for the sins of their fathers? Let's go back to the story of the little boy named Christopher. He was informed that he's going to have to be the one who breaks the curse.

Most people aren't as fortunate to have that responsibility placed on them at such an early age. It gave Christopher enough time to self-fulfill that prophecy. Christopher seems to be the only one who has the spirit and ability to change his family's future. He's gifted and talented, and he doesn't want future generations to go through the same struggles of past generations, whether it's personally, financially, or business related. He's determined to break the mold for generations to come and has the desire to retire his parents when he makes it.

Throughout the years of seeing both wealthy people and poor people, I decided that it is better to become wealthy so that you can lift others higher and remove the bondage and baggage they carry in the lives. It should be in every man's heart to leave a Godly legacy for his children and their children. I encourage every young man and woman to leave this earth a better place for your family and for others. Wanting to break the mold is inspiration given by God and it starts in your mind. Where the mind goes, the body follows. Lead the path to where you want your body to go and bring those with you who want to change their circumstances.

Chapter 10
WHY WASTE TALENT?
"There is One Leadership Quality That Will Make or Break You-
- PURSUIT."

Challenge Your Intellect

I figured this concept out when I was drawing and painting at an early age. I started to feel like there was more potential inside of me and drawing and painting pictures didn't feed my passion. Being a creative person, I couldn't stay in a box and live in a dimly lit world of boredom. As human beings, our minds need to be challenged, that's how they become sharper and more valuable to us. I simply wanted to challenge my intellect, so I left the class to fulfill my dreams.

Keep Your Commitments

When finding something that captures your heart, something that aligns with your future, and gives you the urge to move on, be sure to stay committed to it. Passion is just like a relationship; if your man or woman doesn't show that they're committed, you will lose interest and begin searching for someone who will fulfill your desires. Likewise, stay committed to whatever you're passionate about so that you don't waste the talent that could change the world.

Hold on to Responsibility

Trying to confine your talent is like putting locked bars on how far you can go. Remember, passion can take you places. Use it to the best of your ability. There were times when I took on huge projects and workloads because with my drive and ability, I knew that I could get the work done because I work well under pressure. Has there ever been a time when you took on a responsibility, then realized it was a last-minute type of situation, but you had to get it done? We all have those moments at some point in our lives. As long as you achieve favorable results, holding on to certain responsibilities is okay.

Never Fail to Lead

While growing up in church and then becoming a young entrepreneur, I started to see a pattern. In business, I learned that when you inspire people, you inspire them for a *lifetime*. Songs in church, the environment, the congregation, the pastor and saving souls are what grows the church and empowers the people. That applies in business as well. When you lead a crowd, they will tend to stay with you because they know, like and trust you. However, if you fail to lead correctly, your talent will find leadership in another place.

Never Fail to Care

Emotions are what build people up or tear them down. Throughout the course of life, many people fail to understand the difference between "personal" and "business." However, never fail to care for that individual because they can still respect and follow you. Emotional levels differ. But if you don't care at all for people when doing business, they will eventually leave you. It doesn't matter what talents you have, gifts, money or freedom that you can provide. Touching a heart first is always better than lending an insincere hand.

Break Through to Your Passion

Some people have found their passion or something they love to do. But most people can't figure it out. There are successful people all around the world who have stayed locked inside their rooms with the door shut, and everything else didn't matter because they eliminated all distractions. When people can't seem to find something, they are passionate about, it makes me wonder if they ever had a mentor, or even been around driven people who will point out what they are talented at so they can use it to help others and profit from it. You have to get to a certain point in your life where you realize you want to become better each day and become the greatest at what you do.

Your Contributions

Having great mentors and soaking up their wisdom and advice is critical to learning the ropes of business. One of my mentors explained to me the importance of staying under the radar. There are many people that would love to take all the credit, have all the fame, but that isn't what makes a great leader. A great leader gives his team all the credit for their hard work, loyalty, and diligence. Great businessmen are always under the radar, still going after what they're passionate about. However, they put together a team of qualified individuals who can get more of these things accomplished. It was once explained to me that the greatest man who walked this earth had a team of 12, so what makes us think we can do everything by ourselves? When you don't recognize the contributions of others, you're simply asking them to give you the credit and leave.

That Inner Voice

Many entrepreneurs and businesspeople have what it takes to win in this world by acting on their thoughts, ideas, and insights. It's very few who really listen to that inner voice that gives them confirmation that it's time to make it happen. If you don't listen to that voice, I promise you someone else will.

Discover Your Purpose

Have you discovered your purpose and what you're really supposed to do in life? Do you have a clear understanding of your calling? Many people go through life without finding their true purpose. You'll find what's right for you when doors begin to open, or slam shut. Either way, when defining your purpose, you have to figure out who you *are* by what you *are not*.

Chapter 11
MENTAL SUCCESS STRATEGIES

You may have heard the saying, "You can lead a person to the well, but you can't make them drink." I have heard many people say they have big dreams, but their actions show me otherwise. Reflect on the following mental strategies, take ownership of your success so far, and really start applying the knowledge you learn to your future actions.

William E. Lee Jr.'s Mental Success Strategies:

Find your niche:

Once you find what is best for you, it's always good to stay in your own lane and let your team of people use what works best with their gifts and talents. As entrepreneurs, never become a jack-of-all-trades, but a master of none.

Make good decisions:

Surround yourself with people who are successful and already making good decisions. Understand that "You are the equivalent of the five people you hang around the most." People who are good resources for you will push you to the next level, while people who are liabilities will push you back to a previous level. Always make good decisions and have invaluable mentors in your circle.

Be legitimate:

Always make sure you have your business set up properly so that nothing shows up and surprises you down the road. It's good to have a legal team and a team of consultants so that you're not trying to make decisions on your own. If you have a team of people who are specialized in their field and can give you the blueprint, you make an educated decision from there.

Strive to learn everything there is to know:

I've heard this saying plenty of times, "If you are the smartest person in the room, you are in the wrong room." You may know a few things, but you will never know everything there is to know. But it doesn't hurt to strive to know. As one of my mentors taught me, "we have two ears and one mouth," which means keep your ears open and lips closed. Learn everything you can. Knowledge is great and it will promote you.

Shorten TV time:

There's a time and a place for everything. You can take that to the bank. Always shorten your time from watching television because it can become a distraction. On a regular basis, I make sure that I don't have the TV on while I work. If I do, I have the volume muted so that I won't be distracted.

Become a positive thinker: Avoid people who think negatively and surround yourself with people who lift you up with words. Instead of saying you can't do something, it's too much, or you don't have what you need, find a way to think positively. Say, "I have what it takes. I will find a solution to my problem. I can do this."

Chapter 12
DAILY AFFIRMATIONS

Everything we think, hear, and say is an affirmation. Either you're speaking positive things into your life or negative things that will keep you stuck in a rut.

What do you want in life or business?

Take about 20 minutes of your time to look at your life and consider the things you currently believe. If you feel you are missing pieces of your life and/or business, write that belief down and speak into existence what it is you are missing. Doing this will reprogram your mind to create and accept abundance.

For example: Susan wants to change her mindset and start a business. However, she isn't surrounded by positive people who support her vision. Susan believes it is time for a change and is ready to take massive action. To get started, she can listen to motivational audio daily and create a list of positive affirmations. A few affirmations she could use are listed below:

Susan's Powerful Affirmations for Life & Business

- Today, I have started my journey in creating my own business and taking massive action.
- Every day, I am changing my circle of friends, replacing them with people who see my potential and enlarging my territory.

- I make sure I give the best by providing good value, service, and making sure every client is satisfied with my service.
- I am persistent in my business decisions.
- I am successful and lend help to those in need.
- My business produces massive profits more and more each day.
- I allow surplus in my steps.
- I am focused throughout my day.

Susan can create this simple list of affirmations for herself and repeat them aloud every day.

Powerful Change

Now you will start to experience a change in your thinking and a change your steps. Things will come easier to you because you're speaking positive things in the universe that gravitates to your commands. But you still must take action. I'm sure this is something you will not have a problem doing. All of these changes assure that you don't waste the talent that can take you to the next level in life.

I learned these things from one of my mentors, and now I say my positive affirmations at least three times a day:

- Every morning after I shower
- Before I start working
- At the end of the day or late at night

Remember, this is your moment, the peak of your season.

Make a difference and prove it can be done by your decisions, dedication and determination. Improve your life, help others avoid mistakes, be different, and someone will want to sow seeds of growth into your life. Someone helped me. Now I want to help you. Why waste talent?

Break the mold and leave a legacy!

Take care,

William

ABOUT THE AUTHOR

Dr. William E. Lee, Jr. is the founder and partner of Lee's Press and Publishing Co. LLC, an online premiere self-publishing services company. He also owns a trucking company and is part of a multitude of other businesses and sits on various boards. A young 36-year-old entrepreneur himself, talented, and gifted. Mr. Lee's desire is to inspire and make an impact on the lives of others. William started his own economic development nonprofit with his lovely lady Danielle to serve local workers and entrepreneurs in the area of his hometown, Reidsville NC.

In 2011, William was nominated, along with six additional great men, for the "Just for H.I.M. Affair", and was blessed to be the recipient of the "Hardest Working Man in North Carolina Award". William has since then dedicated his life to helping other entrepreneurs and executing business ideas.

Mr. Lee was also nominated and selected to receive the Prestigious 2021 Honorary Doctorate degree in Humanitarianism. He has written this best-selling book entitled, Breaking the Mold – Why Waste Talent, a book that sheds light on his upbringing, principles everyone can follow to overcome and how to use your gifts and talents to create a successful business.

William has been called with a purpose to help others avoid mistakes and live a life of value. He was the first in his family to attend college after dropping out of high school in 2004. He has mentored and counseled youth in the community and has spoken across the country to various high schools and colleges. William's mission is to leave a Godly Legacy for his family and generations to come.

www.ingramcontent.com/pod-product-compliance
Lightning Source LLC
Chambersburg PA
CBHW071913070526
44583CB00016B/1968